Calligraphy

THE EASY WAY

By Diane Foisy

Thank You

Calligraphy THE EASY WAY

This edition published in 2013
By SpiceBox™
12171 Horseshoe Way
Richmond, BC
Canada V7A 4V4

First published in 2008
Copyright © SpiceBox™ 2008

ISBN 10: 1-77132-015-X
ISBN 13: 978-1-77132-015-3

CEO and Publisher: Ben Lotfi
Author & Calligrapher: Diane Foisy
Creative Director: Garett Chan
Art Director: Christine Covert
Design & Layout: Charmaine Muzyka
Production: James Badger, Mell D'Clute
Sourcing: Janny Lam, James Xiong
Photography: Howard Prendergast Photography And Dreamstime stock images on history pages 8-17 and Dover pictorial archives for illuminated art samples on page 56.

For more SpiceBox products and information, visit our website: **www.spiceboxbooks.com**

Manufactured in China

3 5 7 9 10 8 6 4 2

CONTENTS

INTRODUCTION

You are about to embark on a journey into the age-old art of calligraphy. For over twelve centuries, people have been using this beautiful writing style to lend importance and elegance to documents of all kinds, from bibles, law texts and decrees, to modern awards and wedding invitations. Now you too will be able to create timeless documents written in the calligraphic style.

Your guide in this journey is professional calligrapher Diane Foisy. Her simple and easy-to-follow teaching method will help bring out your innate ability to learn and, with lots of practice, help you master the skills to write in the Chancery hand.

As with the calligraphy students she works with one-on-one, Diane takes you through the letters of the alphabet one pen stroke at a time, encouraging you to master each individual portion until everything looks just right. She then gradually builds your skills until, before you know it, you've gone from individual strokes, to letters, and then on to whole texts. She provides you with tips and tricks to make sure that your ink flows well, your pen is kept in good condition, and even shows you some sample designs and projects to get you started.

In a fast-moving world where printing presses and computers have overtaken the art of beautiful handwriting, calligraphy is an anchor. As you learn, you'll also notice how much your friends and loved ones enjoy receiving your handwritten creations, how they impart a certain value to your notes, invitations and gift tags, and how special they feel to receive one of your creations.

So, enjoy learning calligraphy. Practice is the key. Take your time, and take pleasure and find relaxation in each step. Be sure you feel comfortable with each pen stroke before you continue to the next. Before long, you'll be fashioning your own beautiful pieces using this unique art form.

CALLIGRAPHY:
What does this word mean?

Calligraphy comes from the Greek word kalos which means "beautiful" and the Greek word graphein which means "to write." In other words, "beautiful writing." If you look up the word calligraphy in a dictionary, you'll see it can refer to both beautiful penmanship and to handwriting in general.

Where Did Calligraphy Originate?

Throughout time, humans have looked for ways to represent and record the significant events in their lives. It can be said that the art of calligraphy has been developing since the beginnings of art itself with early cave paintings. As mankind developed, so too did the art of drawing pictures.

In about 3500 BC, the Egyptians created the highly stylized system of hieroglyphics for which they are well known. These symbols were carved inside tombs or painted with brushes across papyrus paper. Around 3100 BC, the Sumerians of Mesopotamia developed a series of pictograms for keeping track of measurements and weights in order to conduct trade more easily. It replaced the ancient system of counting stones and drawing animals. The pictograms were simplified over time and became abstract forms, much like some common symbols that we use today, such as @, #, $, %, & and +. The Assyrians and Babylonians adapted the Sumerian symbols for their own use.

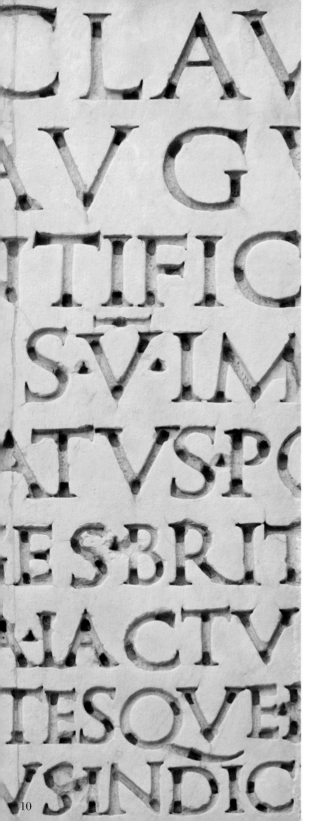

About two thousand years later, around 1200 BC, the Phoenicians, a civilization whose land followed the coast in what is now Lebanon, Syria and Palestine, went a step further and developed what is believed to be one of the first alphabets. The Phonetic symbols replaced the drawings and any concept could now be expressed by a combination of symbols or letters. The Hebrew alphabet was derived from the Phoenician and neither alphabet contained vowels. Through maritime trade, the Phoenicians spread the use of the alphabet to North Africa and Europe where it was adopted by the Greeks and Etruscans.

By 850 BC the Romans had adapted the Phoenician form of writing to suit their Latin language. With the spread of the Roman empire, and its eventual conversion to Christianity, Latin became the universal language of the churches of Europe. During the Middle Ages monks began to carefully scribe copies of ancient religious texts into decorative books used by high-ranking Church members and royalty. Paper was expensive during the Middle Ages, so the scribing monks developed a writing style that was narrower, allowing more words to fit on a single line. Thus the Gothic lettering style was born. It lasted as a popular scribing technique throughout much of the Middle Ages.

By the mid-15th century, Johannes Gutenberg had invented the printing press, and its lettering was based upon the Gothic lettering of the monks. The invention of the printing press allowed for faster printing of bibles and so threatened the occupation of the monks. However, although the use of the printing press spread worldwide, handwriting skills were still in high demand. The printing press was no replacement for handwritten everyday letters, formal correspondence and invitations.

As the arts flourished during Europe's Renaissance, so too did the art of calligraphy. During this time, the Italians invented the italic script, which became popular throughout most of Europe. The 17th century saw the arrival of engraved copperplates, which permitted the printing of finer lines more suited to printing the italic script. In a short period of time calligraphy became an endangered art and by the 18th century artistic penmanship was in a steep decline.

arts flourished and so did the art of calligraphy...

19th-century artist William Morris spearheaded a calligraphic revival.

To further complicate matters for artistic scribes, by the 19th century the steel pen and fountain pen had replaced the flat-edged pen. The rounded tip of these new pens made the special curves of calligraphy more difficult to achieve. The art itself might have seen its extinction had it not been for the British poet and artist William Morris. In the mid-19th century, William Morris, who was one of the principal founders of the British Arts and Crafts movement, a pioneer of the socialist movement in Britain and a well-known designer of wallpaper and patterned fabrics, spearheaded a calligraphic revival. He reintroduced the flat-edged pen, returning the act of writing to the art form it had once been.

It might seem that the art of calligraphy couldn't possibly withstand the competition from the 20th century's most important invention — the computer — with its wealth of fonts and options, allowing you the choice of style you want, all generated electronically and printed in an instant. But calligraphy is flourishing with calligraphic societies throughout Canada, the United States and Europe.

Why has calligraphy stood the test of time?

Calligrapher, Julian Waters, noted during a lecture at Washington's Sidwell Friends School in 1997 that true calligraphy is the art of producing letters that capture the spirit of the text they represent. For many artists, much mental pre-planning is necessary to fully understand the text before deciding how to display it in its full beauty. This type of emotion cannot be generated from a computer, which for Julian Waters is "simply another tool" to be manipulated by the artist.

Calligraphy is a popular art form whose boundaries are not restricted to Canada, the United States and Europe. Around 1500 BC the Chinese developed a complex writing technique that uses more than 1,500 characters. Today, the Chinese consider calligraphy to be one of their most respected art forms. Master Chinese calligraphers may appear to be spontaneously stroking a brush over the paper, but many meditate extensively before designing.

愁腸化作相思淚
人睡明月樓高休獨倚酒
鄉魂追旅思夜夜除非好夢留
　　　情更　　　　　

15

Ottoman Calligraphy on a mosque wall

Persian is a language with a long and rich history that dates back more than two millennia. The written form, which includes eighteen distinct shapes and is written from right to left, gradually developed into an art form. Arabic script appears highly distinctive from the lettering used throughout most of Europe, but they have many Greek and Phoenician influences in common. In Arabic calligraphy there are six major scripts — Farsi, Naskh, Kufi, Deewani, Req'aa, and Thuluth — representing various artistic styles.

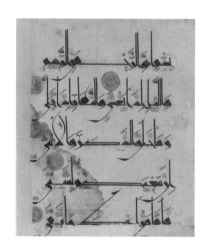

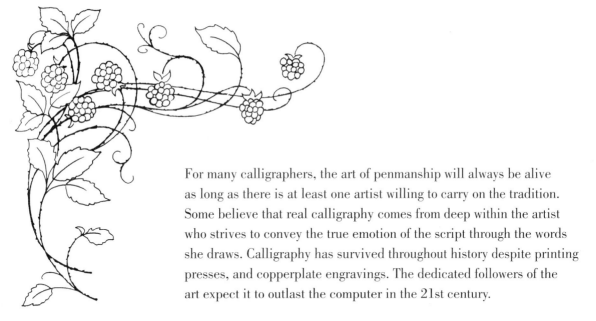

For many calligraphers, the art of penmanship will always be alive as long as there is at least one artist willing to carry on the tradition. Some believe that real calligraphy comes from deep within the artist who strives to convey the true emotion of the script through the words she draws. Calligraphy has survived throughout history despite printing presses, and copperplate engravings. The dedicated followers of the art expect it to outlast the computer in the 21st century.

History has shown us that calligraphy will prevail.

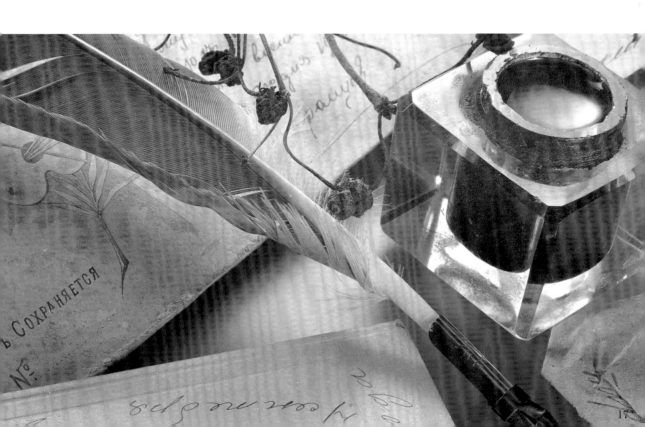

EQUIPMENT
Basic Materials

Before you begin, be sure to have at hand your calligraphy pen along with different nib sizes — fine, medium, and broad; a bottle of ink or ink cartridges; lots of inexpensive paper (i.e., bond paper); paper towels or a blotter; and a small container of water. Now you are ready to begin.

Choose a drawing board or any table surface that suits you. Your work surface should give you lots of space in which to move your hand freely.

Care of Your Pens and Nibs

1

Care of the pen's nib is important. Always flush it out with water before putting it away. This will give the nib a longer life, prevent it from clogging and make it ready for use the next time you pick it up.

2

Once you have the ink cartridge attached to your nib or the pen's chamber filled with ink, have at hand either a paper towel or an ink blotter to get the ink started through the nib. Just place the nib against the paper towel or ink blotter, and pull the nib towards you until the ink is flowing out.

3

Remember, you always pull the nib towards you while working with it. The pulling motion draws the ink through the nib. If you use a pushing motion, the nib will catch on the paper and splatter ink. It is also very hard on the nib.

THE BASICS

Figure 1

This is always the beginning stroke. You should never move the pen in your hand. It should always be kept at the same angle on the page. Practice many rows of this stroke. Use an inexpensive bond paper to practice these basics. It's best to use unlined paper. If you begin to learn calligraphy with lines you will find you come to rely on them. By practicing on unlined paper, you will develop your eye for straightness.

While doing these basic strokes, if the ink does not flow, correct the angle until you have the stroke like the sample shown. You will develop a feel for when the ink flows well. Continue to do this very basic stroke until you have consistency as shown here in Figure 1.

Once you feel comfortable with this stroke and you are achieving consistent results, you are ready to go on to the next step. Make this beginning stroke again, and now add another stroke, straight down. It will look like Figure 2.

Do many rows of this until you feel comfortable, and achieve the look of the sample consistently.

When you feel you are ready, go on to the next step. Do the first angle stroke, bring the nib of the pen straight down and add another stroke, straight across along the bottom.

It will look like Figure 3. Again, do many rows of this until you can recreate the look of the sample consistently.

Figure 2

Figure 3

Figure 4

Move on to the next step, doing all the previous strokes and adding this additional stroke. It will look like Figure 4.

Do the rest of the following sequences to the right: Figures 5, 6 and 7 (as shown with the straight E, F, H).

While learning these very basic strokes, always begin with many small strokes to be sure that you have the nib on the page correctly and at the proper angle, with the ink flowing from the nib. Once you have it, do not change the position of your pen in your hand in any way. Imagine that it is taped to your hand. You will find that once you master these basics in calligraphy, you will be able to create any lettering style.

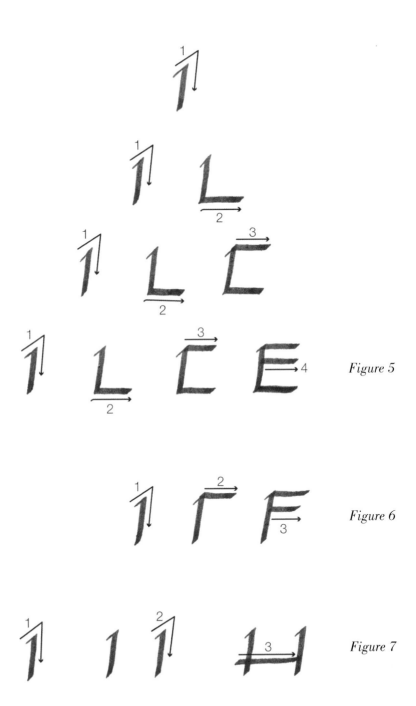

Figure 5

Figure 6

Figure 7

A B C D E F G H
I J K L M M N
N O P Q R S T U
V W X Y Z

a b c d e f g h i j k l m n o p
q r s t u v w x y z

1 2 3 4 5 6 7 8 9 10

Figure 1

I will show how to construct each letter by breaking it down into individual strokes. I will also show the directions of each stroke. Putting these together will give you the letter.

For "I" start with the little curve, as shown. Keep the angle of the nib the same as the beginning stroke, and go up slightly, along and up at the end. There is a slight curve here, but the eye will see it as a straight stroke across (Figure 1).

Do many rows of this. Once you feel comfortable with it, and you are achieving consistent results, add the second stroke, which is straight down from the middle. The bottom of this stroke should have a 45° angle. Then add the third stroke, going up a little, then angle down slightly and up at the end. You should see an opening from the end of the second stroke to the finished third stroke. This opening would be seen showing the angle of the second stroke to the third stroke.

Instead of following alphabetical order, you will learn the Chancery lettering style by learning to do the letters from the simplest to learn, to the most challenging. Once you have mastered the upper-case letters of the Chancery style, you will find it very easy to do the lower-case letters in alphabetical order and the numbers.

Note: Do all the lessons in the sequence given, as this is a step-by-step method to success.

Practice the rest of the letters, following the arrows for each stroke that I have outlined for each letter. Each stroke is a building block used to construct the complete letter.

Note: If you find any part difficult, go back to the basic first stroke, making sure your pen angle is correct and that you are getting a good flow of ink as you pull the nib along the paper. This stroke is very important, as it applies to each and every letter. The angle must not change. If your work appears uneven, correct the angle of the nib.

Once you feel comfortable with this stroke, return to the letter you were last doing well, and come forward step by step, stroke by stroke, until you reach a level of comfort again.

Be sure that you are not rushing yourself. Have patience and remember that you are learning each and every stroke well, before you go on to the next step.

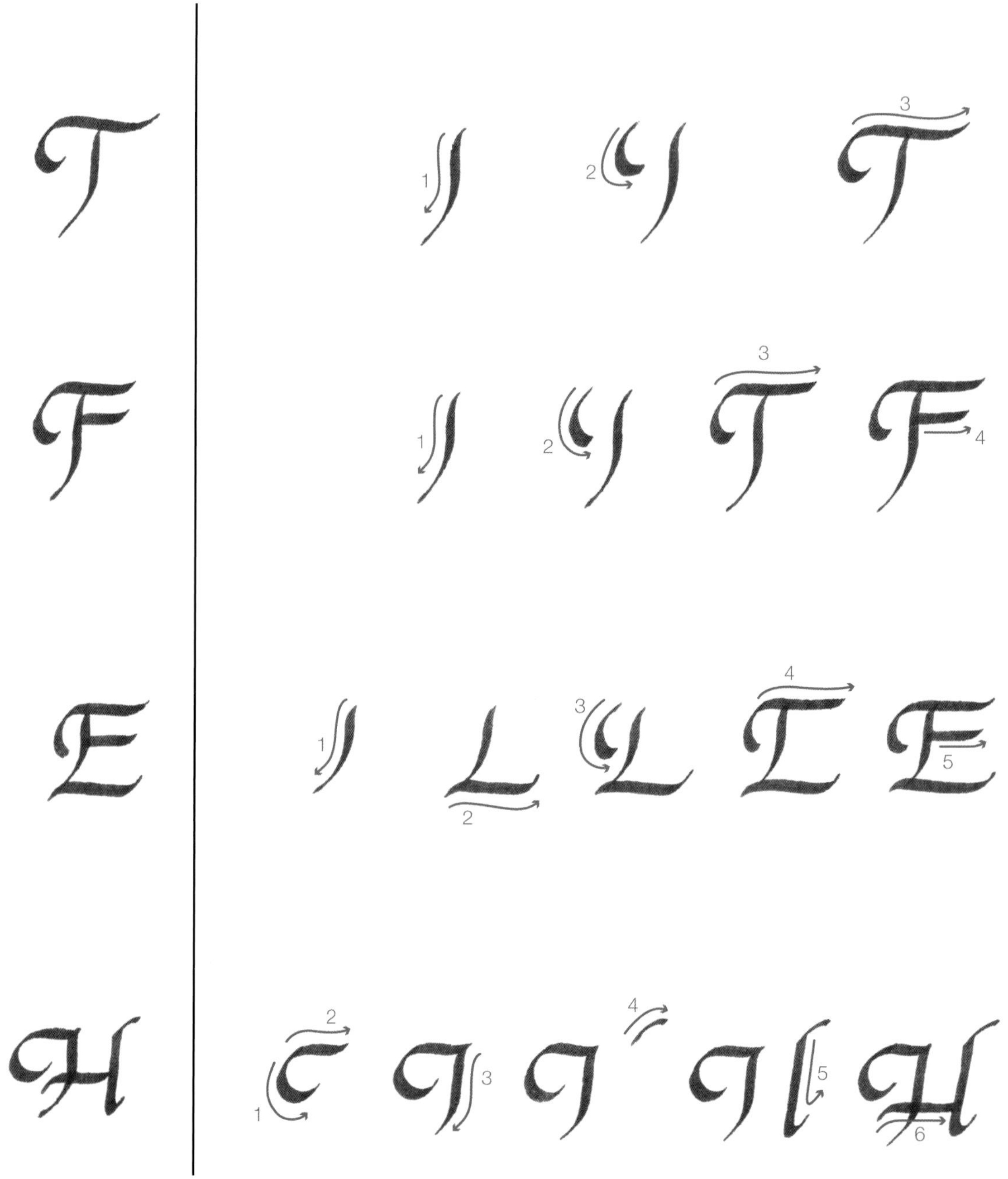

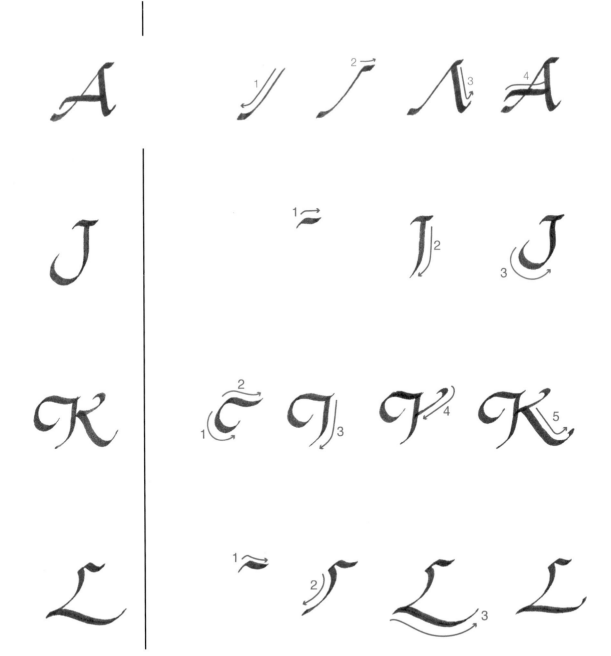

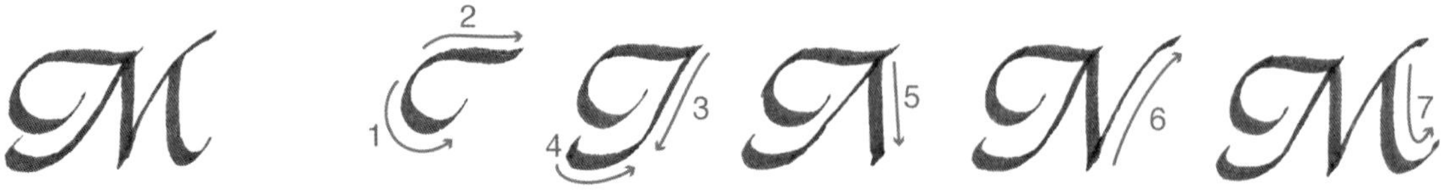

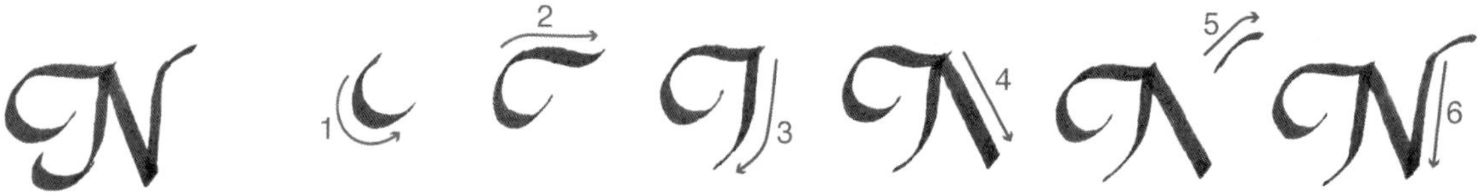

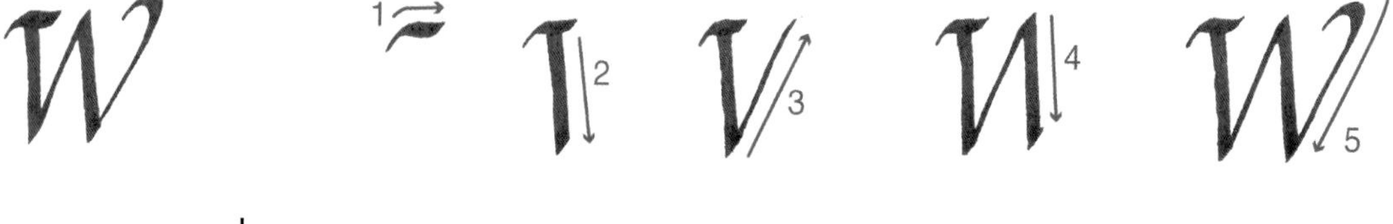

x

u

y

z

e

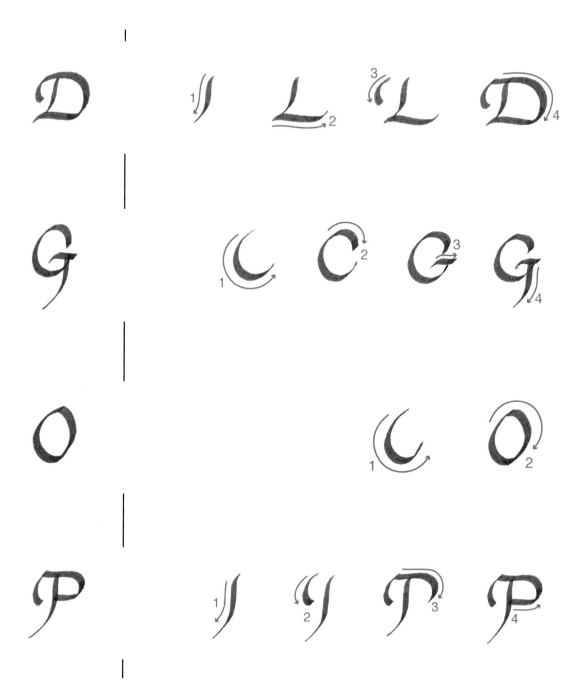

Q

C O_2 Q_3

R

J_1 J_2 T_3 P_4 R_5

S

1 2 S S S_3

B

J_1 L_2 L_3 P_4 B_5

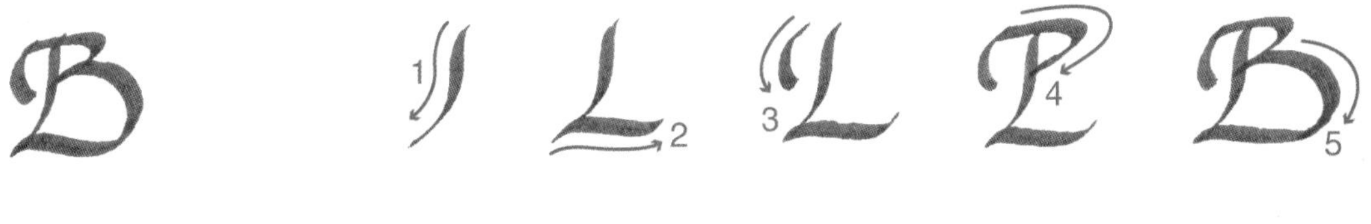

33

a

b

c

d

e

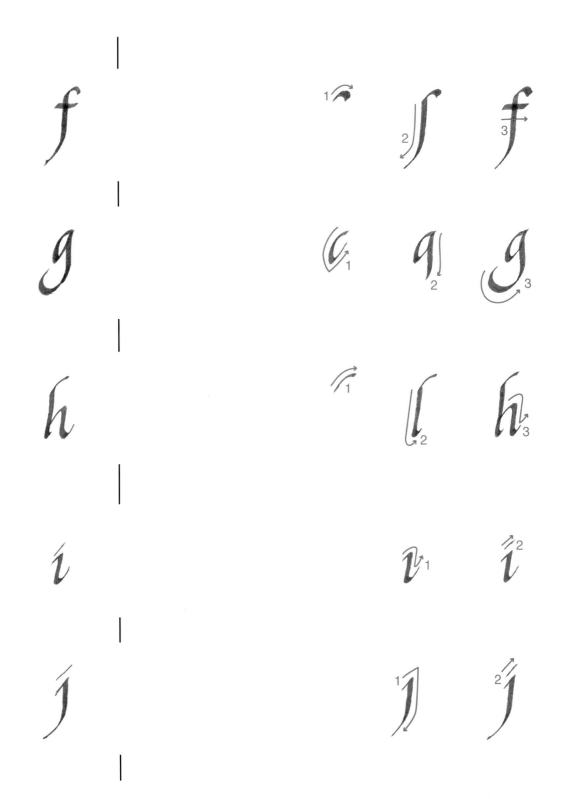

k

l

m

n

o

p   1 p 2 p 3

q   c 1 q 2 q 3

r   r 1 r 2

s   1 s 2 s 3

t   l 1 t 2

u v_1 u_2

v v_1 v_2

w v_1 v_2 w_3 w_4

x v_1 x_2

y v_1 y_2 y_3

z ^{1} z_2 z_3

1

2

3

4

5

6

7

8

9

10   [1]1

SPACING
Spacing of Letters

You have now completed the alphabet, learning to write both the upper-case, or capital, letters of Chancery, and the lowercase, or small, letters. Now we'll move on to putting the letters together to form words. To do this well, you need to look at the balance of the whole word. There is no measurement involved, just a visual judgement of where to place the next letter so that it looks even. The letters should not be crowded in one spot or have too big a gap between letters. Practice will help you to achieve this, and with lots of practice you will be able to do this consistently.

Let's have a look at the word "recipes." I extended the front stroke of the "r" below so that angle gave it the balance it needed. The next letter, "e," is not that close to the "r," as the angle of the stroke from the "r" takes up space. The "e" is one of the fuller, more curved, small letters so you need to allow space on the left side, as it is right beside the extended angle of the "r." That is where you place it. Next is the "c." It should be placed fairly close to the "e" because of its shape and the space it takes up. Make sure when you are creating and placing the letters beside one other that you are looking at the height of the letter, keeping in mind where it begins and ends so that it lines up with the previous letter. This is where straightness without use of lines is achieved, along with maintaining consistent size and height of the letters used to create the word. The letter "i" is very skinny, so you need to allow more room on each side for it to look balanced with the rest of the letters.

The "p," "e" and "s" are fairly close together as they are rounded letters that take up more space. Once the word is done, the word as a whole should be balanced. Your eye should not be stopped by any crowded spot, or by letters that are too far apart and cannot be read properly.

Practice many words until you are satisfied that you have achieved the balance needed to combine the letters to form words with an even appearance throughout.

Spacing of Words

Now that you are able to form words with even placements of letters, we will combine the words to form sentences, so that the body of your calligraphy communicates evenly.

Create letters one at a time to form words just as you learned in the previous lesson. Allow space between the words so that each word can be easily read and the spacing between the words is even. Avoid creating areas where the words become crowded or the gaps between the words too big.

The use of calligraphy gives a beautiful aesthetic finish, whether it is a letter; an invitation; a document; a poem; or an address on an envelope. The completed piece becomes a paper treasure for the recipient.

Projects

NOTECARDS

Notecards make lovely invitations, thank-you cards or place-setting cards. They can be used to give any occasion that special elegance.

Before working with your notecard, decide how to best place the words on a separate piece of paper. Practice it a few times, until you have the look you want for the notecard. Note how you'd like to have the words spaced, and ensure that your message will fit on the paper size you've chosen. Once you have established how you'd like the words to look, you can move on to creating the real thing. Using your practice sheet as a guide, you now know where to begin based on the amount of space required to place the message on the notecard. In this notecard, I simply wrote the words "Thank you."

WINE BOTTLE TAGS

These make excellent personalized holiday gifts or hostess gifts, or can be used to acknowledge any celebration by placing your own message on the tags. A personal message done in calligraphy makes a gift that much more special. Take the time to do the calligraphy. It is always very well received.

In this example, I simply wrote "Enjoy your new home." Whatever message you choose to write, practice it on a separate piece of paper to establish the layout of the words in the space allotted on the tags. Once you are happy with the way your message looks, do the calligraphy on the tags themselves. In this case, I centred the word "Enjoy" and then placed the rest on the second line.

SPECIAL INVITATIONS & ENVELOPES

To create invitations, practice your message on a separate piece of paper. You'll see from your practice sheet where you'll need to begin each line of text to centre it on the final invitation. Be aware of your spacing on the horizontal and vertical planes to ensure all the text will be easily read on the final invitation.

In the sample shown here, I have featured a wedding invitation. It's best to keep the wording of the invitation itself simple. I want to place the emphasis on the names of the bride and groom. To achieve this, I have arranged for their names to be a bit bigger and more ornate. The rest of the information is kept smaller, and is communicated simply and clearly. Keep in mind that while calligraphy should be beautiful, it also needs to read well in order to communicate a message.

Once you've written the invitation, attach a bow and trim it, making sure the ribbon is not covering the message on your invitation.

You now have a beautiful invitation your guests will rave about. Hand-done calligraphy sets the tone for a wedding, or any other special event you are holding.

Mr. and Mrs. David _
431 Oilard Boulevar
Toronto, Ontario
M5R 2V1

Together with their parents
Emily Rose Olson
&
Michael G. Waylon

invite you to share in the joy
and celebration of their marriage
on Saturday, the seventeenth of May
two thousand and ten
the afternoon

The favour of your reply is re
by April 17th

M _____

_____ accepts _____

Ms. Jennifer Hayes
432 Jane Avenue
Toronto, Ontario
M5A 2V1

TAGS & LABELS

Practice the names of your tags and labels on a separate sheet of paper as you did with the other projects. The smaller space on hand-done tags and labels can be challenging to work with, so take your time and practice a number of times before working on the final tags or labels. As you can see, I was able to decide where to place the words and the end result is well balanced on the tag.

Once you have established how the name done in calligraphy will look on a separate sheet, you will know where to place the words. Here I wrote "Ribbon & Trim." These tags and labels can be used for gifts, in photo albums or on jars in your kitchen. Here I used the tags for baskets.

FRAMED QUOTES

Practice writing the body of the poem or quote on a separate sheet of paper. Leave a space for the first letter. The first letter will be done larger and more ornately, so allow room for the additional size and decoration. Allow space between the lines for added flourishes.

Once the body of the text is done, you can see where to extend strokes to add flourishes to the body, filling in the spaces. Do not add too many, otherwise the text will become distracting and difficult to read. You will get a feel for what is pleasing to the eye, where to place these flourishes, and when to keep the writing simple.

You can take one of the templates included in this book and add the swirls along the bottom, along the side or wherever you want them to be. You can do these in different colors if you choose. I placed the swirls at the bottom centre. I used black for the central part of the design and gold for the extended swirls towards the outside of the design.

I took the first letter "L," filled it in with gold, and made it a larger version of the Chancery-style "L," adding a little curl to the top of the "L." Have fun with your creations and add your own flair and personality.

$\mathcal{L}$ove looks not with the eyes,
but with the mind;
and therefore is winged
Cupid painted
blind."

ILLUMINATION

The monks in the monasteries added illuminated art to their manuscripts during the period of about AD 800 to AD 1200. Monks wrote the text and included painted illustrations as added decoration. Through their art, the monks expressed their interpretations, religion, as well as philosophy, law and other subjects. These works of art added importance to the body of text and sometimes depicted the events described in the text.

Sometimes the Renaissance artists would paint a frame in the borders of their paintings, featuring flowers, leaves and vines, done in green, blue, gold and red.

You can have fun exploring the art of the Renaissance era. Try taking a letter, and adding flowers, vines, green leaves, or other shapes, working in and out of the letter, as if it were a trellis.

Here is an example of what I did with a letter. Remember, you are the artist and there is no limit to what you can do to create these decorative letters and borders.

DESIGN TEMPLATES

I have included some design templates in this book for you to play with. You can photocopy the designs onto blank pages. Once you have copies of the designs you want to work with, there are a number of ways to work with them. For example, you can take a graphite stick or HB pencil, rub it across the back of the design and flip it back to the front of the design to trace it out. The design will now appear on your finished piece. Another way of tracing your design is to set the template over a lightbox.

How you finish the designs is completely up to you. You can add paint, colored inks, gold, copper, silver, or anything else you like. Have fun and enjoy working with designs.

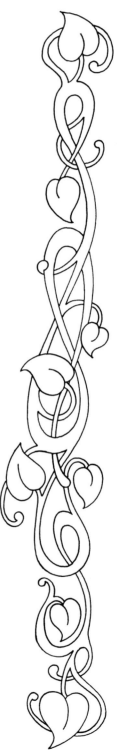

ACKNOWLEDGMENTS

My parents, Guy and Denise Foisy, of Sault Ste. Marie, Ontario, have always encouraged me in my love for the arts and so I would like to acknowledge them here for their unconditional love and support for all that I do.

Many thanks to my beautiful daughter, Janice, and her husband, Alex. Janice is not only my daughter, but also my very best friend, supporting me always in my endeavor to be successful as a calligraphy artist. Thank you, Janice, for providing me with sunshine with your presence and the presence of your beautiful daughter, my granddaughter Ariel, who loves to spend time with me in my art studio.

Many thanks to my husband, Mario Iannuzziello, and his lovely family for their love, and their support and encouragement for my calligraphy services business.

Thank you to my brother, Paul, and sister-in-law Pam, who have always shown a great interest in my calligraphy services; the growth of my business; and who have enjoyed their private lessons. Thank you to all my friends who have encouraged me throughout the years. You know who you are.

Thank you to all my clients, old and new. It is a privilege and an honor to service you. I am very grateful for your ongoing support and referrals.

Thank you to all my students who share my love and passion for calligraphy. Continue to practice and pass on those skills to others so that calligraphy will never be claimed as a "dying art."

Special thanks also to Ms. Susan Waller who cares for my hands and manicures them.

Finally, I want to acknowledge the great resource of the modern age, the Internet, which I used extensively while researching the history of calligraphy and illumination in this book.

Write on,

Diane Foisy

GLOSSARY

Hieroglyphic(s): A picture or symbol representing an object, idea, or sound, as in the writing system of the ancient Egyptians.

Illuminations: Decoration by means of lighting.

Papyrus: A type of writing paper made from reeds by the ancient Egyptians.

Trellis: A cross-barred structure or panel of wood, metal or other material, used as a screen or a support for vines or other plants

Lightbox: A container with several lightbulbs and a pane of frosted glass on top.